L is for LOVE and LIGHT

the new ABC book
encouragement for the child in all of us

written and illustrated by **Sara Page**

Published by
The Open Life

Smithton, MO   www.LiveLifeOpen.com

My hope is that this book will help you to stay true to yourself, and follow your dreams!

Sara Page

Founder of The Open Life

Original artwork, articles, and additional product information available at:
www.LiveLifeOpen.com

Text and Illustrations copyright © 2015 by Sara Page

All rights reserved. No portion of this book may be reproduced in any form without the permission of the publisher, with the exception of brief excerpts in reviews.
Watercolor paint was used for the illustrations.
The text types used are Candara, Century Gothic, Freestyle Script, and Corbel.
Published by The Open Life
Printed by CreateSpace
CreateSpace, Charleston, SC
Available from Amazon.com and other retail outlets
Available on Kindle and other devices.

ISBN: 0692374388
ISBN-13: 978-0692374382

Introduction

This is what you're going to find
This book is not like any other kind.
It's unique, and special, just like you,
And this is what I want to do...
with you.

Let's talk about life in a whole new way.
What if life is a road that we travel each day?

Or what if life is like the wind? We could go fly a kite.
Or if love is like a light, we can shine ours bright.
If life is a game, I want to play with you.
If love is like dreaming, then you're a dream come true!

If life is like an ocean, let's ride this wave.
Let's dance on the water, come on! Let's be brave.
Let's travel this road.
Let's never give up.
Let's DREAM BIGGER than big,
and let's never ever stop.

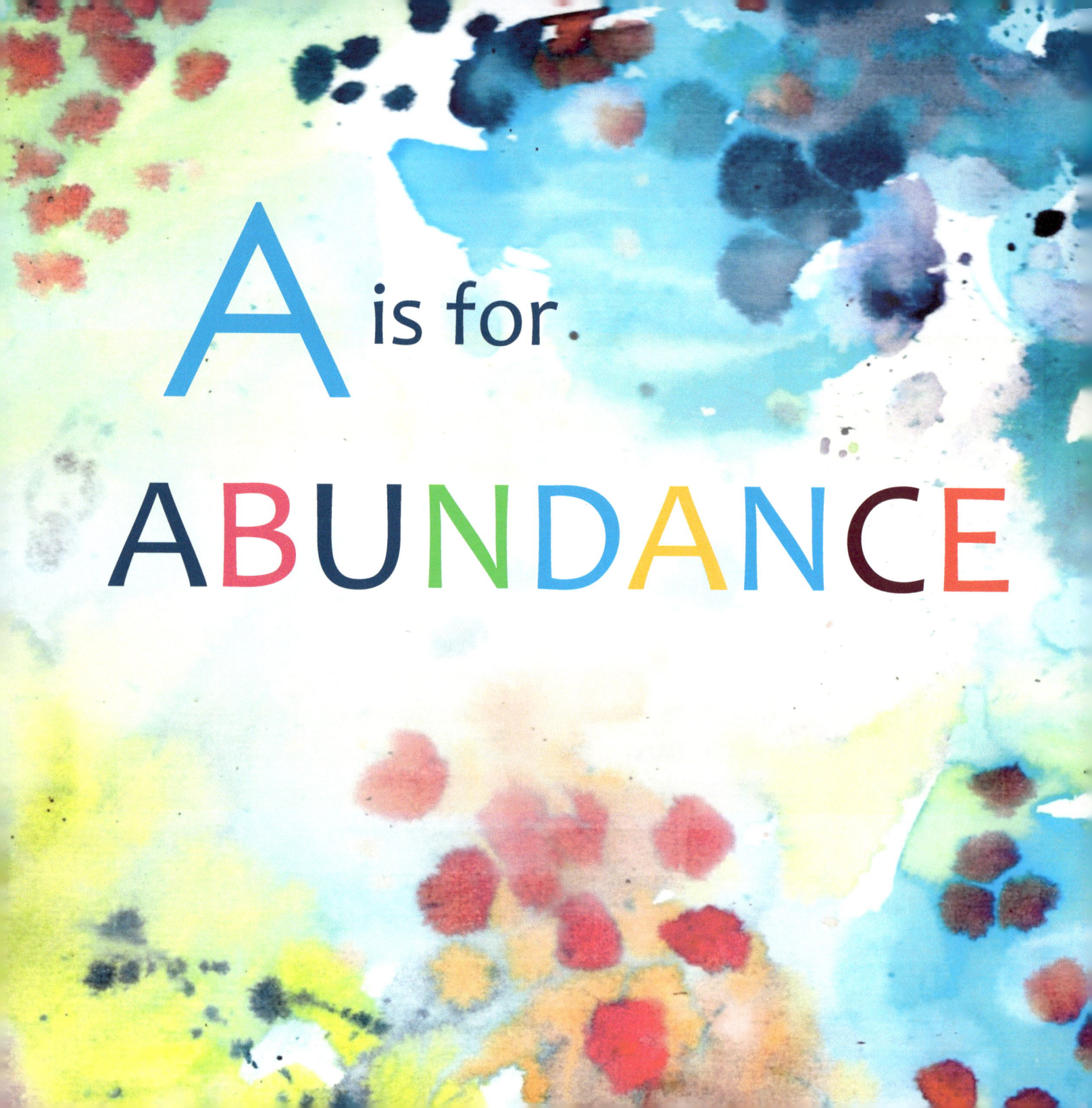

What does ABUNDANCE mean?
**It means that there is more than enough
For everyone to get what they need.**

Like food, and clothes, and houses. Don't worry, you'll be fine!
There's bunches and bunches of the things we need,
and **LOTS AND LOTS** of time.

The UNIVERSE is **BIGGER** than we can even see.
Just trust that you're taken care of, and it's okay to receive.

And when you do, be thankful!
You can't imagine what's in store.
**Celebrate the bounty,
and know there's always more.**

Let's say this together:
*I am thankful that I have what I need,
and I am grateful for the kindness that I am shown.*

B is for BELIEVE

This may not sound like anything
you've ever heard before,

but **choosing what you THINK and BELIEVE**

is a choice that's only yours!

So Believe that anything is possible.
Believe in others and yourself!
Believe that this world is a marvelous place
Believe you're like nobody else!

Believe that you are supported.
Believe you have all that you need.
Believe that growing to *fabulous heights*
Begins with just one tiny seed!

Let's say this together:
**I choose to believe in what INSPIRES me,
and I don't rely on others to tell me what to believe.
I believe in myself, and anything is possible.**

You are unique, and you have a special HEART.
You show us who you are with your smiles, and tricks, and art!

**Even when you're scared,
and you want to run and hide,
COURAGE means you stay,
and you show us what's inside!**

And if you feel worried,
just take some time to breathe.
Tell the ones you love how you feel, and what you need.

Show this crazy world boldly who you are!
Keep on going forward, and I know that you'll go far!

*Let's say this together:
I may be afraid sometimes. Everyone feels afraid!
Even when it is hard to do, I show who I am!*

Close your eyes and breathe.
What do you see? What do you want?
WHO do you want to BE?

Now listen to your HEART. What do you hear?
It's whispering a secret, it says "Don't listen to your fear."

Imagine the ways that your dreams can come true
There's a beautiful world, and it's waiting for you!

So follow your DREAM
Think of all you could do.
Make up a dance! Or play something new!
Never give up, and whatever you do…

Be brave, and just be the real unique you!!

Let's say this together:
I'm making my dreams come true. I believe I can dream big and
_____

(Tell me your dream! You can say absolutely anything!)

E is for

ENOUGH

Just as YOU are, you are good enough.
There's nothing to prove.
What you do is enough.

…Really.
There is enough. You have what you need.
You have what it takes to follow your dreams!

You actually have MORE than ENOUGH.

You might have to get creative,
But that's the fun stuff.

So ask questions, work hard, and remember, think **BIG**.

The world is just full of **possibility**.

Let's say this together:
What I do is good enough. I am good enough. I can find enough of what I need.
I am creative, and the world is full of possibility.
I have what it takes to follow my dreams.

You're wondering what the world's all about.
You have the FREEDOM to ask questions and doubt.

You have your own thoughts, you want us to hear.
You have the FREEDOM to say what you feel.

It's ok to wonder. It's ok to doubt.
It's ok to say what you're thinking about.
Speak from your heart. Do what you like to.
You have the FREEDOM to find what excites you!

Learn about yourself; discover what you like.
Say what you want, and be brave with your life!

Be your own person, and soon you will see.
It's all up to you, so choose to be FREE!

Let's say this together:
*I choose to be Free. I have the FREEDOM to ask questions
to find out more about the world, the FREEDOM to ask for what I want,
and the FREEDOM to say what I feel!*

ABUNDANCE means that there is more than enough. (*We have everything we need.*)

GRATITUDE is noticing the abundance we receive.

Gratitude is being **thankful**
for the delightful things in life.
A friendly smile, a helping hand, a sunny day, or a peaceful night.
We can be thankful just for being alive...
we can even be thankful for the bees in the hive!

What are you thankful for?
_____
(*You can say absolutely anything!*)

Let's say this together:
I notice when someone is kind to me,
And I make sure to be thankful for the gift of kindness.
I have GRATITUDE for the ABUNDANCE of beautiful people
and beautiful things I get to see every day.
This world is amazing!

Do you sometimes feel sad?
Like you're out there all alone?

Like your HEART is broken?

Like you're on your own?

I know that life is hard; it can surely take it's toll.

**But your heart is not broken.
It's complete. And whole.**

You don't have to feel this way **ANY LONGER**.
(*The funny thing about your heart is it's really getting stronger.*)
You are bigger than this sadness.

You are LOVE without an end. Your HEART knows

this is TRUE. (Let it be your trusted friend.)

Let's say this together:
*My heart is complete and whole. I listen to my HEART,
and I trust what it knows is true.*

What do you want?
How do you want to feel?
How will you get there?
What will make it real?

Your INTENTIONS make your life.
They're the way you choose to live.
When you choose to live from your heart,
You have so much joy to give.

When you live your life this way, your LIGHT inside will show!
You can bring your own happiness, wherever you go.

And when you live your life happy,
Then life becomes a game.
And you INSPIRE others that they can do the same!

Let's say this together:
I will choose how I think and act in my life.
I will set an example for others.

There's not much better feeling

than doing what you LOVE.

You DO it just to DO it. You DO it "just because!"

Focus on that feeling; when you're floating on a cloud…
That's excitement! That's adventure!
That's living life out loud!

But things aren't always happy,
so if right now, life's not fun… That's ok!
We all feel sad sometimes, like we just can't find the sun.
When you play the game of life,
sometimes you lose, sometimes you win.

Stay OPEN to learning all you can,

and find your JOY within.

Look for sunshine. Acts of kindness. Notice the unique!
Joy is all around you, if it's what you seek.

Let's say this together:
I use my free time to do what I LOVE to do. I find joy deep in my heart.

Be KIND to others.

Be KIND to yourself.

With a generous heart, be of comfort, and be of help.

Show some compassion.

Reach out your hand.

Listen to others **with your** HEART
to show you understand.

Let's say this together:
I listen with my Heart. I try to listen closely so I understand.
I look for ways to be kind to myself and others.

True LOVE is like LIGHT
It's CONSTANT and BRIGHT!
It's deep in our hearts.
(That's where it starts.)

Can't lose it, or find it, can't ever change it.
(It's always with us, it's part of our greatness!)

It's **acceptance of others** just as they are
It's forgiving somebody, not starting a war.

LOVE can't be bought, Or "fallen into"…
It's something you **are,**
And it's something you **do!**

Let's say this together:
I am made of LOVE and LIGHT. LOVE is always with me,
deep in my HEART. I share my LIGHT with the whole world.
I am connected to everyone in the Universe.

M is for MINDFUL

The mind is so busy. Find some time to be silent.
Like right NOW you're alive, are you calm? Are you quiet?

Now think of your surroundings, do you ever do this?
Just relax? and just feel? and just listen? and notice?
The sounds, the smells, the feel of your chair.
Or the feel of your legs, your arms and your hair.

MINDFUL means being aware of your thoughts

Aware of your body; aware of your socks!
That might sound silly, but just notice how
your feet and toes feel, how they feel right NOW.

When you're eating, just eat! Stay calm, **pay attention.**
The food is so yummy; you don't want to miss it!
And any time you're feeling lots of different feelings,

**You can calm yourself;
just focus on your breathing...**

This is key to your WELLNESS, as simple as it may seem:
Just notice how it feels, being a human being!

**Can you be OPEN
to trying something new?**
(Here are some things that you could try or do)

New food
New drink
NEW *way to think*

New lessons
New games
NEW *friends and their names*

New color
New style
NEW *reason to smile*

*Tell me, is there anything new or different
that you would like to try?*
_____
(What's something new? You can say absolutely anything!)

I open my ears to listen...
I hear the birds as they **sing**.
I open my eyes to see;

I can see a brand NEW thing!

I open my mind to the lesson; I won't turn AWAY.
I'm open to learning more,
so OPEN I will stay.

I open my heart to forgive... it's easy
to offer LOVE.

Every day is a NEW beginning...
I'm choosing to rise above.

Let's say this together:
My life is open, my heart is open, my mind is OPEN.
I am OPEN to learning and seeing NEW and awesome things.

Listen for a moment.
Breathe in.
Breathe out.

Take a big breath.
Breathe in.
Breathe out.

Find your quiet place…
This is your PEACE

Find your still place…
This is your PEACE

All is perfect. All is well.
Just be patient. Just be still.
Stay right here in the present moment.

Let's say this together:
I am Peaceful inside. I can breathe and find my Peace.
A peaceful life begins with me.

Why do we ask questions?
To find the ways that we could go,
and learn about each other
things we'd like to know.

The world is full of questions,
(I'm sure you have a few.)
Some of them I'm certain
you will find the answers to.

But there are just some QUESTIONS
no matter how hard we try,
we never find an answer
(like its hidden in the sky)

So leave some things to mystery.
You know all you need to know.
You have everything you really need
To move on down this road

Let's say this together:
I have the freedom to ask questions. I accept that some questions don't have answers, or that the answers might come later.

When someone is mean, or treating you bad
How could you not start to get mad?
But what they say and do is not up to you.

You control only the things that YOU do.
First take a breath, and wait just a second.
Try to relax… Could you ask them
a QUESTION?

You might find out something that you didn't know.
But whatever they say, you can just LET IT GO!

When it's time to RESPOND,
You stay calm as you speak. With kindness
and PEACE, You just say what you think.

Let's say this together:
In every situation, I will choose to RESPOND with kindness and peace.

When you smile, you
SHINE your LIGHT!
We love that smile, so
shine it bright!

In the dark, SHINE that light!
Love this world
with all your might!

Don't think twice;
Don't wait one more day!
We need that light to
SHINE the way!

Let's say this together:
I am Special. I am Unique. I SHINE my Light for all to see!

What do you
know is true?
What do you say
is true for you?

You are LOVE. I believe that's TRUE.

(How do I know? Because I'm LOVE too!)

You are strong. I can tell!
You belong. All is well.

YOU are creative. YOU are FREE!
YOU can be anything you want to be.

Let's say this together:
I know what is true. I am love, I belong. I am creative, I am strong.
I can be anything I want to be! I am Free!

It seems nothing ever stays the same.
It's kind of "Up and Down."
The seasons change, our teachers change,
we grow, and move around.
Even still, we're all connected;
Everyone is in this together.

The UNIVERSE never stops
being creative… It's eternal.

Some things in life are UNIVERSAL

They never stop. They're eternal.
They are here for everyone.
They are true, and last forever.

PEACE, LOVE, and LIGHT; JOY, and FREEDOM!
We can find them anywhere, as long as we stay
OPEN.

Let's say this together:
I can find Peace any time, anywhere. Things in my life might change, but I still have Freedom. Some things, like LOVE, LIGHT, and JOY never go away.

Sometimes when you dream, **THAT** dream's just for **YOU.**
Good dreams are amazing, those dreams can come true!
But what would you say is your hope for the planet?
How could life be better for everyone on it?

We all have our DREAMS;
deep down we're the same,
but some dreams grow so big, It's a whole different game.

This is called VISION

and it can **CHANGE THE WORLD**
Everything that's brilliant started with a boy or girl
who grew up with a dream that they hoped
would come to be, and that dream became a vision
bringing good to you and me!

So what is your **GRAND** VISION?
What do you hope to see?
Ask, and try, and never give up,
and it could come to be!

Your body matters.
It's worthy of care.
You are unique from your feet to your hair.

WELLNESS

means watching your health from the start.
The health of your mind, your body, and your heart.

What do you eat?
How do you move?
(How does it feel when you get in your GROOVE?)
When do you rest?
After you play?
Be KIND to your body… every day.

Let's say this together:
**I am kind to my body. I love my body and
I am proud of the things my body can do.
I take care of my body and my mind.**

is for eXciting!

Life is always changing...
a new experience each day!
Be present in the moment,
'cause adventure's on its way!

Life is so eXciting!
There are lots of ways to have fun...
If nothing else, just be alive;
go outside and soak up the sun!!

Y is for
YOU

YOU are learning, YOU are growing.
You are more than OK.
YOU do big things, YOU try so hard
every single day.

You're expanding your awareness
of yourself in all you do.

Its crazy and eXciting;
You're the expert on you!

Do you know, that YOU can be
anything you *want* to be?

You are *precious,* this is TRUE...

I see the LOVE and LIGHT
in YOU!

Z is for ZESTY and amaZing, too!

Art backgrounds on these two pages by: Lily and Maya

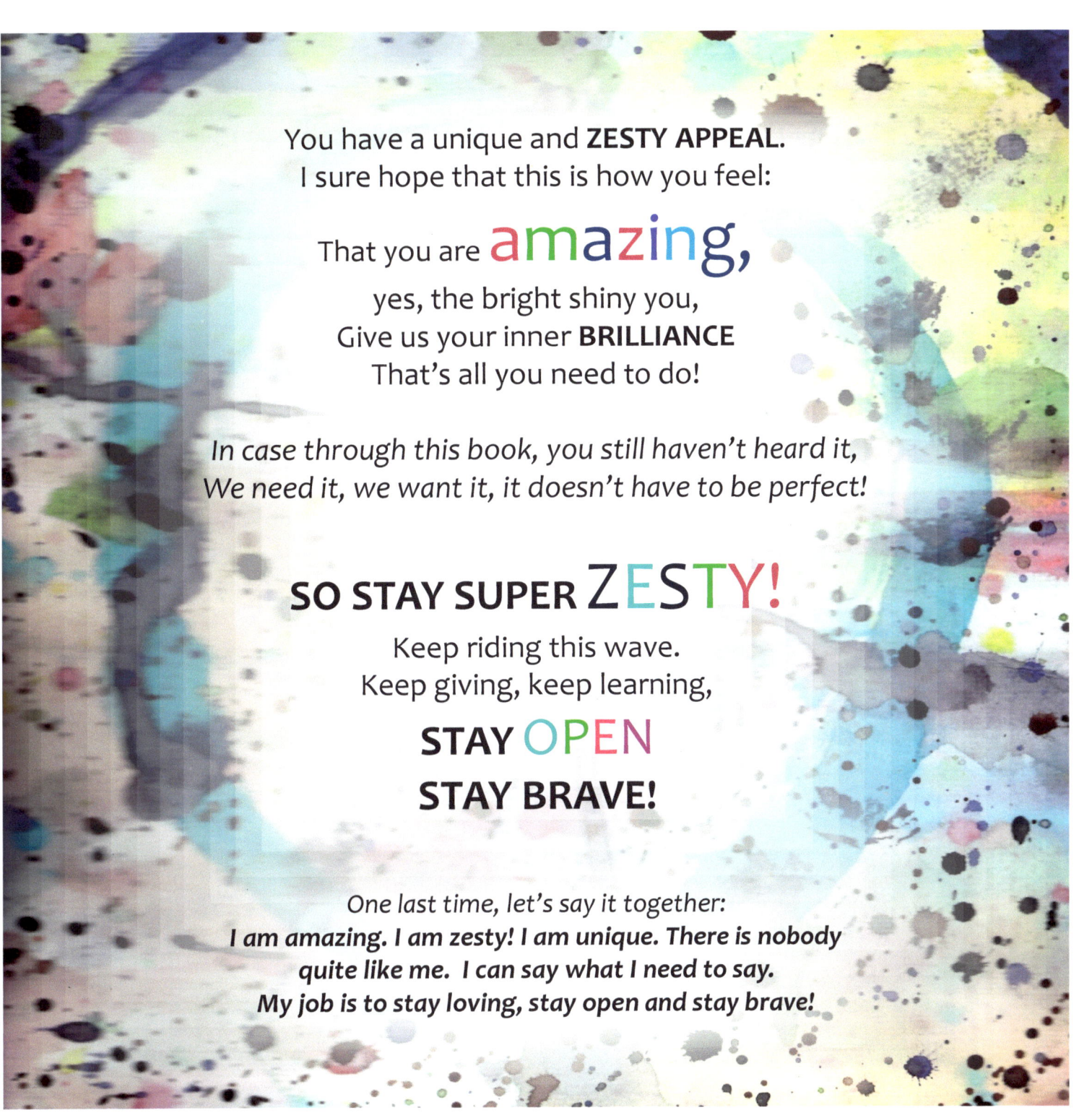

You have a unique and **ZESTY APPEAL**.
I sure hope that this is how you feel:

That you are **amazing**,

yes, the bright shiny you,
Give us your inner **BRILLIANCE**
That's all you need to do!

In case through this book, you still haven't heard it,
We need it, we want it, it doesn't have to be perfect!

SO STAY SUPER ZESTY!

Keep riding this wave.
Keep giving, keep learning,

STAY OPEN

STAY BRAVE!

One last time, let's say it together:
I am amazing. I am zesty! I am unique. There is nobody
quite like me. I can say what I need to say.
My job is to stay loving, stay open and stay brave!

L is for LOVE and LIGHT

A is for ABUNDANCE

B is for BELIEVE

C is for COURAGE

D is for DREAM

E is for ENOUGH

F is for FREEDOM

G is for GRATITUDE

H is for HEART

I is for INTENTION and INSPIRE

J is for JOY

K is for KINDNESS

L is for LOVE and LIGHT

M is for MINDFUL

the new ABC book
encouragement for the child in all of us

N   is for NEW

O   is for OPEN

P   is for PEACE

Q   is for QUESTION

R   is for RESPOND

S   is for SHINE

T   is for TRUE

U   is for UNIVERSAL

V   is for VISION

W   is for WELLNESS

X   is for eXciting

Y   is for YOU

Z   is for ZESTY and amaZing too!

C is for CREATE

my very own ABC book
(the book you write yourself)

Concept by **Sara Page and Diane Burnett**

Published by The Open Life
Smithton, MO   www.LiveLifeOpen.com

Now it's Your Turn!
Buy the Companion Workbook, and CREATE YOUR OWN!

C is for CREATE: my very own ABC book

If you could pick a word for each letter in the alphabet, what would you choose? What do you like? What words inspire you? What words remind you of who you are? H could be for Happy, A could be for Awesome! Or maybe T is for Tiger, and N is for Nebraska! Who knows? Only you do!

Now you can create your very own ABC book!
Order today: it's the book you write yourself

Book includes 52 pages of creative space, where you can make your book your own. Structured like "**L is for Love and Light**", only without the words or text… just the letter! To start, answer some questions about your book, and find words that have meaning to you. Make it your own with pencil, pen, marker, or crayon. Or maybe cut out images and words and glue them in! Also includes a short list of words that start with each letter to get you started. The sky's the limit; there are no right answers here! Get additional help from a dictionary, thesaurus, or use some of your favorite books for inspiration! This is a fun project you can do by yourself, or gather a group of friends and do it together!

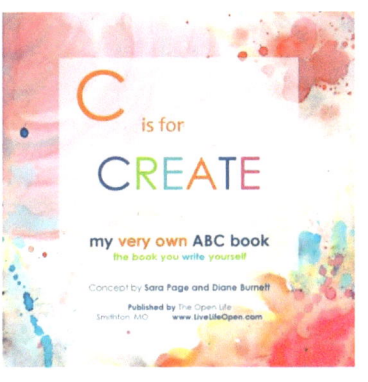

Look for our publications on Amazon.com and through other retail outlets, or visit The Open Life's website for additional product information, plus original artwork, articles, and resources.

www.LiveLifeOpen.com

The purpose of The Open Life is to inspire people of all ages to stay true to themselves, find the courage to live from their hearts, and Live Life Open!

Sara Page
Artist, Writer, Catalyst for change
Founder of The Open Life
Pictured here with daughters, Lily and Maya

Hello!
Thank you for picking up this book! My passion is helping people find the courage to live from their heart, and this book is my way of doing just that!

A little about me...
I graduated from Truman State University, where I majored in Art and Marketing. After living in St. Louis for 11 years, I returned to my hometown of Smithton, MO. I have an awesome supportive group of people in my life that I get to call family and friends.

I have a website called The Open Life where I share my art, my thoughts, and my various creations. (I'm into a lot of different things!) Come visit me there, and if you do, leave a message or a comment and tell me about you!

My website:
www.LiveLifeOpen.com

Visit for additional product information, plus original artwork, articles, and resources. Keep up with the latest when you sign up for email updates!

Notes

Notes

www.ingramcontent.com/pod-product-compliance
Lightning Source LLC
Chambersburg PA
CBHW041945110426
42744CB00027B/15